Faith @ Home

God's Gifts for Growing a Great Family

Michelle Waters

CSS Publishing Company, Inc.
Lima, Ohio

FAITH @ HOME

FIRST EDITION
Copyright © 2014
by CSS Publishing Co., Inc.

Published by CSS Publishing Company, Inc., Lima, Ohio 45807. All rights reserved. No part of this publication may be reproduced in any manner whatsoever without the prior permission of the publisher, except in the case of brief quotations embodied in critical articles and reviews. Inquiries should be addressed to: CSS Publishing Company, Inc., Permissions Department, 5450 N. Dixie Highway, Lima, Ohio 45807.

Scriptures taken from the Holy Bible, New International Version®, NIV®. Copyright © 1973, 1978, 1984, 2011 by Biblica, Inc.™ Used by permission of Zondervan. All rights reserved worldwide.www.zondervan.com. The "NIV" and "New International Version" are trademarks registered in the United States Patent and Trademark Office by Biblica, Inc.™

Library of Congress Cataloging-in-Publication Data

Waters, Michelle.
 Faith @ home : God's gifts for growing a great family / Michelle Waters. -- FIRST EDITION.
    pages cm
    ISBN 0-7880-2789-1 (alk. paper)
 1. Parenting--Religious aspects--Christianity. 2. Child rearing--Religious aspects--Christianity. 3. Families--Religious aspects--Christianity. 4. Families--Religious life. I. Title. II. Title: Faith at home.

BV4529.W37 2014
248.8'45--dc23

2014012711

For more information about CSS Publishing Company resources, visit our website at www.csspub.com, email us at csr@csspub.com, or call (800) 241-4056.

e-book:
ISBN-13: 978-0-7880-2790-1
ISBN-10: 0-7880-2790-5

ISBN-13: 978-0-7880-2789-5
ISBN-10: 0-7880-2789-1   PRINTED IN USA

*To
Samuel Curtis
David James
Jonathan Thomas
Matthew Benjamin*

Table of Contents

Introduction   7

Chapter One   11
Living Together in Little Churches: The Gift of Family

Chapter Two   19
Living in Conversation with God: The Gift of Prayer

Chapter Three   27
Living in the Word: The Gift of the Bible

Chapter Four   33
Living the New Life: The Gift of Baptism

Chapter Five   39
Living in Communion: The Gift of Forgiveness

Chapter Six   45
Living with Purpose: The Gift of God's Best

Chapter Seven   51
Living a Family Culture: The Gift of
    Doing Things Differently

Chapter Eight   57
Living for the Lord: The Gift of Legacy

Introduction

The baptism is over. Your little bundle of joy made it up to the altar without too much trouble. She probably squirmed a bit, maybe threw an all-out fit. Nevertheless, the pastor welcomed her into the family of God and the congregation looked on with pride.

Now what?

As parents, we make all sorts of promises on behalf of our children at the baptismal font. If your pastor used a traditional liturgy, you vowed to bring your child faithfully to a house of worship, teach him the Lord's Prayer, the Creeds, and the Commandments, and at the proper time, place in his hands the Holy Scriptures… so that he may lead a godly life until the coming of Jesus Christ. Not only is that an incredibly daunting responsibility, it's the most important work God has given you as a parent. Put simply: raising your child in the faith is now your number one priority.

At least it should be.

Unfortunately, many of us have turned this great responsibility over to the "officials." We want the Sunday school teachers to work miracles in the one hour we give them each week. If it doesn't happen there, we expect the youth workers to go a little further and take our children on a mission trip. As a last-ditch effort, we hope the young adult ministry will reach our children before it's too late.

Shocking as it may be, you will not find the words "Sunday school teacher," "youth worker," or even "theological scholar" in the Bible. What you will find is a simple structure that God has always used to transmit the faith from one generation to another: the family. Parents living the faith as little eyes look on.

For many parents, this is an intimidating — if not terrifying — task. During my six years in ministry at a large Lutheran church, I can't tell you how many times parents told me they felt inadequate to deal with their children's questions about God. And these were very young children — even preschoolers — whose questions were both simple and sincere. It's not that these concerned parents couldn't come up with an answer that would satisfy little souls: It was the perceived weight of the consequences. What if I'm wrong? What if I say something silly? What do I know, anyway?

I often taught classes on baptism and communion — the former for fourth graders pledging to be prayer partners for their newly baptized brothers and sisters in Christ, the latter for fifth graders preparing to come to the Lord's Table for the first time. The fourth and fifth graders sat dutifully, rolled their eyes a few times, stumbled over the Bible verses I asked them to read, and hoped this would all come to a speedy end.

Not so with the parents. Ordinarily quiet-in-the-pews moms and dads were bursting with questions, grasping for anything that might make their director-of-faith-at-home job a little easier. Their anxiety was palpable. They wanted a formula: What if he asks this? What do I say to that? What do we believe about baptism, anyway? Many lined up to speak with me afterward, grateful that they got a "refresher course" on basic Christian beliefs.

These parents understood firsthand that the culture our children encounter is no longer predominantly Christian. In large part, our children encounter messages hostile to the faith from all directions — some are direct attacks, some much more subtle. We cannot expect an hour here, or a retreat there, to completely alter the worldview they are fed day-in and day-out in schools, on TV, and online. It is up to us as Christian parents to reclaim our primary role as purveyors of the faith and make our homes "little churches."

There is nothing new here. In the beginning, the church was established by believers "and their entire households" (Acts 18:8). Luther, in the sixteenth century, was dismayed and discouraged that parents did not know enough basic theology to properly teach their children about the Lord. His Small Catechism was addressed to the head of the family and written for the purpose of household instruction. Catholic doctrine emphasizes the home as the domestic church where father, mother, and children exercise their baptismal priesthood in a privileged way.

To be entrusted with so great a task — ushering another soul into the arms of the Savior — is indeed a privilege. It is the most natural, beautiful expression of faith and the most difficult. While the culture continues to push our children aside — as the disciples did so many years ago — Jesus continues to say, "Let the little children come to me, and do not hinder them, for the kingdom of heaven belongs to such as these" (Matthew 19:14). It is our job, as the guardians of young souls, to make sure they can hear his call and respond to his love with an open and pure heart.

It is my sincere prayer that in these pages you find hope and encouragement for the road ahead. May God bless you with grace sufficient for all your days.

CHAPTER ONE

Living Together in Little Churches: The Gift of Family

The Bible tells us that "God sets the lonely in families" (Psalm 68:6). How beautiful! God created us first and foremost for relationship with him, but in his wisdom and grace he gave us human relationships to help us grow in love, patience, and compassion here on earth.

Sadly, because of sin, often what is intended as a gift becomes a burden. Many families hardly see each other — with parents working more and more hours and children overextended by academic and extracurricular activities outside the home. Teaching children anything meaningful about a relationship with Jesus Christ is almost impossible in such harried circumstances.

On top of that, our society views children as accessories: sometimes cute, sometimes inconvenient, always optional. We shuttle them off to daycare so we can find fulfillment in work outside the home. We hire others to teach them to swim, dance, play baseball, and read — exchanging the all-important role of parent for the drudgery of being a chauffeur and director of activities. We bow down to the "experts" in all sorts of circumstances, when we alone know the real hopes, dreams, and needs of our children.

Parenthood is certainly not glamorous. There are messes to clean up (constantly), noses to wipe, diapers to change, and attitudes to adjust. There are lots of tears to dry, manners to teach, and fights to break up. It is not easy and comes with little outside praise.

Adding insult to injury, the media is no friend of the

family. The sitcom father is always a bumbling idiot. Housewives are desperate. Mothers live meaningless and miserable lives (unless they've chosen to forsake their role completely — then it's all high heels and high glamour). What's worse, the preschool set is served up program after program where there is no parental involvement in the main character's life at all. When my daughters were young, they asked me why Dora got to run around the woods all by herself all the time! If children are fed a steady diet of parent-bashing programs and commercials, it doesn't take long for them to adopt our culture's denigration of the family.

Several years ago, my oldest and youngest children were in the car with me on an errand. We stopped for gas, and inevitably, the baby began screaming at the top of his lungs. An older woman at the pump next to me commented, "You seem so calm even while your baby is screaming." I told her that he was my fifth child and by this point I could handle it. She immediately gushed about how lucky I was, that she only had four children. She was sure it must be so much fun at our house.

The moment I got back into the car, my eight-year-old said, "She must be a Christian."

"Why do you say that?" I asked.

"Because she said you were lucky to have five children. Everyone else is just waiting to get the kids out of the house."

Sad? Yes. An accurate description of our culture? It seems increasingly so.

God has an entirely different perspective. Children are "a heritage from the Lord" (Psalm 127:3). They are always welcomed by Jesus, despite the disciples' desire to turn them away. "Children are arrows in the hand of a warrior" (Psalm 127:4) and the warrior will "not be put to shame when he contends with his enemies in the gate" (Psalm 127:5).

Make no mistake, there are enemies prowling around the gate of the family. There always have been. It's not just the television and the internet that make being a Christian parent so much more difficult in today's world. It's the increasingly secular, relativistic worldview that permeates everything from your child's history textbook to the programs she watches on television.

While this poses real problems in your attempt to teach your children the faith, it also offers you an amazing and beautiful opportunity to model something different in your own home. The door is wide open for your family's small piece of property to become a large mission field.

Dietrich Bonhoeffer, a martyred Lutheran pastor and theologian, called the home a "kingdom of its own in the midst of the world, a stronghold amid life's storms and stresses, a refuge, even a sanctuary."[1] The home is a place where spirituality can and should permeate everything. You have the great blessing and responsibility to tell your children about God at every turn. When your four-year-old bounds through the door screaming because he got stung by a bee and he is asking why God even created bees, you have the privilege not only of drying his tears and comforting him, but of giving him a short sermon on how God cares even for the bees and gave them a way of protecting themselves when they're in danger. You don't have to go into a great scientific lecture on how incredibly important bees are to the entire ecological system. All that is needed is a few words recognizing that God is the one behind it all and we can trust that he knows what he's doing.

When you come together for a family meal you are able to nurture not only their bodies but their souls by thanking God for the food you've received and having fellowship with your spouse and children in the midst of the busy days. Eating together is a small thing in and of itself but the result is

13

proven to be incredibly beneficial and long-lasting. Turning off the phone, TV, and iPad during this time ensures that your attention is on each other and the gift that God has placed before you. Eating the same food in different places — or in front of different screens — within your home doesn't suffice. The Lord has "prepared a table" before you (Psalm 23:5). That's a whole lot different than a couch, a computer desk, or the seats in the minivan.

When your children ask why their rooms have to be kept neat, you remind them that we serve a God not of "disorder but of peace" (1 Corinthians 14:33). Again, there's nothing incredibly profound here. A variety of responses on your part — to any of these situations — would suffice. The objective is nothing more than pointing your child to God in the big things and the small. It's simply a family living out the daily routine but doing it with the Creator of the universe in mind.

Why?

Because how we live out the small moments of our lives eventually becomes the big picture. More aptly put, "We sow our thoughts and we reap our actions; we sow our actions and we reap our habits, we sow our habits and we reap our characters; we sow our characters and we reap our destiny."[2] If the daily cares are given up to God, soon our whole lives will be too.

It is these very small, seemingly meaningless rituals that help aim your "arrows" — the children God has blessed you with — in the right direction. The world is more than willing to blow them this way and that, increasing their appetite for one thing after another. If we don't teach them the ways of the Lord, they will be "blown here and there by every wind of teaching and by the cunning and craftiness of men in their deceitful scheming" (Ephesians 4:14). Remember, there is an "enemy at the gate" just waiting to aim those arrows — your precious children — back at you in an aggressive assault on your family.

So many years ago, Noah faced a corrupt and evil culture. Everyone, everywhere had turned away from God, "every inclination of thoughts of man's heart was only evil all the time" (Genesis 6:5). What did Noah do in such desperate times? He listened to God. He built an ark, not because he was particularly fond of animals, but because he was asked to do so by God. I doubt "wildlife conservation" was high on his agenda. He built the ark to "save his family" (Hebrews 11:7). He built it to give them shelter in the face of the impending storm.

God's call to the Christian family has not changed. The circumstances continuously change. The surrounding culture changes. But the role of the family is still the same: to nurture and protect another generation of world-changers. We can still show our children, our neighborhood, and our community a different way. We can aim our "arrows" toward eternal life in Jesus Christ: "I call heaven and earth to witness against you today that I have set before you life and death, blessings and curses. Now choose life so that you and your children may live, and that you may love the Lord your God, listen to his voice, and hold fast to him" (Deuteronomy 30:19).

Building Your Family's Ark

For many people, home is not a place of comfort and security but of chaos and strife. The mess is ever-present; the laundry continues to pile up, and the quarrels never quit. A few brave parents admit that they would rather be at work than at home — at least there is a sense of order at work and people treat them with respect.

Nothing about raising children naturally lends itself to

order or peacefulness. The very presence of children — even from the first days at home — causes less sleep, more laundry, and quite often stress between the precious bundle's mother and father. As the child grows — and more children join the family — the flurry of activities, the sheer volume of "stuff," and the never-ending to-do list threaten to drown out any sense of family cohesiveness and joy.

Many of us know instinctively that this is not the life we envisioned for our families. We never dreamed our primary role would be chauffeur and cook. We didn't sign up to be queen of de-cluttering. We never knew how much money we could spend just to get ourselves organized!

The "God of order" never envisioned the family to be this way either. His word continually calls us back to the "still waters" of following him. His Son promises day-in and day-out to carry our greatest burdens and relieve our deepest fears. God "*makes* us lie down in green pastures," because it is completely against our nature to do so on our own (Psalm 23:2). Many of us complain continually about the rat race, but when push comes to shove, we're afraid to get off the track.

Turning your home into an ark implies doing everything you can to mitigate the stress caused by the hustle and bustle of daily life "out there." It's about creating an atmosphere completely different. For some this may mean unplugging from the constant stream of "white noise" that typically surrounds us: the drone of the 24-hour news cycle, the beep of the text message, the barrage of advertisements clamoring for our attention. In our family, reducing newspapers to only the weekend and not having cable television have reduced the information overload immeasurably. Getting rid of our landline in favor of cell phones also means not being bothered by solicitors. These are small steps in and of themselves, but they go a long way in maintaining a sense of peace and quiet in our home. Peace and quiet is certainly not the goal. Making room for relationship with Jesus and each other is. If there's no time for conversation, no time for prayer, no time for anything but the increasingly long "to-do" list, there's no hope for making deep and meaningful connections with those around us. Moreover, we've failed to provide a shelter from life's storms for God's most precious possessions: our families.

---

1. Dietrich Bonhoeffer, *Letters and Papers From Prison* (New York: Touchstone Publishers, Simon & Schuster, 1997).

2. C.A. Hall, *The Home Book of Quotations* (New York: Dodd, Mead & Company, 1935), p. 845.

CHAPTER TWO

Living in Conversation with God: The Gift of Prayer

It isn't supposed to rain in the desert. But there we were, vacationing in Arizona with two small children, and the rain wouldn't stop. The girls were getting restless and there wasn't much to do in our little condo. We needed a plan.

We decided to make the hour-long drive to the Phoenix Zoo, hoping that the rain would be done by the time we reached our destination.

As we meandered through Phoenix traffic our pace slowed to a crawl and the rain showed no indication of stopping. The closer we got to the zoo, the more I feared we had made a big mistake. Not only would we miss out on all the animals, we'd have even squirmier children than we started with! They'd been cooped up in the car for over an hour and we would be turning around and doing it all over again!

As we entered the parking lot, the rain pelting our car and dashing our spirits, we decided to pray. We bowed our heads and asked God for a miracle: "Please God, if it is your will, stop this rain so that we can go to the zoo."

We parked the car and started unloading. As we approached the ticket booth, the rain began to stop, the sun started to come out. We were incredulous! The ticket taker looked at us strangely, obviously confused why we would even bother coming to the zoo that day. "You're lucky," he said. "It's been pouring all day and no one's around. You got here just in time!" The girls were able to share with him, very enthusiastically, that it wasn't luck at all but God's answer to prayer.

That day lives on for us in many ways. It was a beautiful testimony that God hears our prayers and sometimes answers them right then and there. We recount it over and over again to remind our children not only of God's great power, but of his great care as well. We serve a God who often wants nothing more than to delight us, his precious children.

The situation would have been completely different if God decided to let the rains continue to fall. We certainly would have been disappointed, and our trip to the condo would have been a somber one. But it would have provided a teachable moment, nonetheless. Our girls would have learned — as they've come to understand through many situations since then — that God doesn't always answer prayer so instantaneously. Often his answer doesn't turn out the way we had hoped. Many times we wait and wait for an indication that God even hears us. There are plenty of occasions when we fail to understand how God is "working all things together for our good" (Romans 8:28).

Nevertheless, the Bible tells us to "recount the wonderful deeds of the Lord" (Psalm 9:1). Reminding your children of family prayers answered — like our miraculous trip to Phoenix Zoo — is one way to do that. Keeping a prayer journal is another. Write down all the people and situations your family is praying for. As time passes, write down how you see God answering those prayers. You can do this orally too, just by reminding your children of what you've been praying for and what God is doing about it. My husband has years of prayer journals lining the walls of his office. His personal prayers are written out in black ink and God's answers to those prayers are added later in red. It's a beautiful witness and record of a life of prayer and a great comfort in times of doubt or discouragement.

Many parents find those few minutes before bed the best time for hearing what's on their children's hearts, and bringing those concerns before the Lord. One way to structure a family prayer time is by simply asking each person one thing they're thankful for, one thing they're sorry for, and one thing they're praying for. After hearing from everyone, gather all these petitions together and bring them before the Lord. It doesn't need to be any more complicated than that. If you're like me, you're exhausted at the end of the day and brevity goes a long way.

Obviously, as parents attempting to raise future men and women of faith, we need to be in constant prayer for our children's hearts, souls, and minds. The world is waiting to snatch them away. Prayer is the vehicle for unleashing God's power on their behalf. While unusual, I know several families who have successfully raised all of their children to be strong believers. This is God's wonderful gift, of course, but these parents certainly played a part in such important kingdom work. The one thing I know for sure all of these parents have in common is that they are devoted people of prayer. They have spent plenty of time on their knees on behalf of their children.

There have been seasons in our family's life when one particular child was in need of more ardent, intentional prayer. This is to be expected: Jesus said there are some things that are only healed through "prayer and fasting" (Mark 9:29). One Lenten season, I took it upon myself to pray and fast during lunch for this child's struggles. Only the Lord knows for sure what was accomplished during those forty days, but the peace it brought me — knowing I was handing this issue over to the Lord — was more than enough to sustain and encourage me through a difficult time.

Becoming a Family that Prays Together

There is no formula, no single right way to pray as a family. The important thing is that your children have a lasting memory of this ever-so-important facet of the Christian life. They need to know that you take all things — big and small — to the one who cares for all the concerns of our hearts. They need to see you "take it to the Lord in prayer" in moments of both joy and sorrow. Even a few words here and there will powerfully demonstrate to your children that God is in control: not you, not them, not the powers-that-be.

Prayer can set a day gone bad back on the right track. Just the other morning, as I attempted to get the children ready for their Tae Kwon Do class and my husband was heading out the door to work on his sermon, there was backseat bickering and a huge helping of bad attitude emanating from our over-sized van. It took only a few words from their father's mouth, directed at the Lord on our behalf, to set things back on track. Nothing profound was spoken, no great motivational speech was uttered. Just a father standing in the gap for his family, reminding all of us that we serve a God of second chances and that even this situation was under his control.

When things begin to go south in our home — something that seems to happen quite frequently when you've got six sinful children and two sinful parents living under the same roof — I've been known to mutter the Kyrie under my breath repeatedly: "Christ have mercy. Lord have mercy. Christ have mercy." When and why I began this habit I can't recall. But all the children who are mobile know to run for cover. Apparently the message conveyed is "Mom can't handle this on her own. She needs the Lord's help. Run!" I can live with that, but I like my children's response to stressful situations better. They've learned (from the fabulous Adventures in Odyssey audio series) to offer up a different petition when someone or something is bothering them.[1] "Count it all joy" is their go-to phrase when the going gets tough or the tension starts to rise. When another drink is spilled all over the table, "count it all joy." When the baby ruins yet another just finished Lego® creation, "count it all joy." And when Mom is surely about to lose it, "count it all joy." The point is that when the little things begin to get under our skin, God reminds us of the big picture: "Count it all joy, my brothers, when you encounter various trials, knowing that the testing of your faith produces perseverance" (James 1:2-3). The take-away lesson for believers old and young is that the Lord bears our burdens and shares in our sorrows; we offer them both to him through prayer. He holds our cares and concerns in his protective, powerful hands.

If you set this example early on, prayer will quickly become second nature to your children. In times of stress or disappointment they will instinctively take their burdens to the Lord. Children are so quick to grasp even the big ideas. Our five-year-old son's current prayer of choice is: "Thank you Lord that you made the ultimate sacrifice for us." Nothing warms a mother's heart quite like hearing such sweet, sincere thankfulness coming from the mouths of her babes. Undoubtedly, we have plenty of less profound prayers ("Thank God for monster trucks!") around our table too. Gratitude, in all its varieties, is an encouragement to all.

It doesn't take long for our children to realize that Mom and Dad aren't in control of the universe. Things go wrong on our watch. Details are forgotten, promises are overlooked, and justice isn't always served. When children understand that you put your trust not in your own fallible power, but in the incomparable power of almighty God, they feel secure and cared for by a heavenly Father who will never let them down and whose love for them endures forever. That's a fairly large return on a pretty small investment.

The Power of Prayer for Parents

Expectations were high as my fresh-scrubbed, Christmas-clad clan made their way to the Christmas Eve services. My husband had left hours before to put the finishing touches on his sermon and deal with the last minute details. I gave my annual speech in the car: "You know how much Mommy loves the Christmas Eve service. It's my absolute favorite part of the entire year. I need a big dose of 'Joy To The World.' So, please, please, please, behave!" I was laying it on unusually thick this year. That should have been my first red flag. Not to mention it was past bedtime for half my brood even before the service began. I'd be sitting alone with six small Christmas cherubs, trying to capture my own personal "Silent Night, Holy Night." It truly is "the most wonderful time of the year," but for a pastor's family, Christmas can be incredibly challenging as well.

It's no surprise that things didn't go well. By the third song, I was outside the sanctuary pacing with two squirming siblings, worrying about how the four older ones were faring on their own. When the ushers passed out the real candles (and yes, they were lit), I was forced to surrender all control to the newborn king.

Once back in the car, a sad silence descended upon us. I had set them up for failure and now they felt like they had let me down. Tears streamed down my face as we drove off into the darkness. Please, Lord, help me.

Not far out of the parking lot, a light snow began cascading from the clear, night sky. "Silent Night" came on the radio. From the backseat, one of my daughters whispered, "Mom, God is giving you your Christmas service after all." More tears — more surrender — more proof that he's the one in control.

"The family that prays together, stays together" may

be cliché, but there's certainly truth to be found there too. It's almost impossible to remain at odds with people you're praying with and for. When we come together to talk to the Lord of all creation, our senseless squabbles and petty preoccupations are put in their proper perspective. When we bring "the hopes and fears of all the years" to him in prayer, we remind our children (and ourselves) that he's got it all under control. Joy to the world!

---

1. Adventures in Odyssey, 1993, album 18, episode 225, "Count it all joy."

CHAPTER THREE

Living in the Word: The Gift of the Bible

> But seek first his kingdom and his righteousness, and all these things will be given to you as well.
> (Matthew 6:33)

Coffee and quiet — those are the first things I need every morning. Believe me, it's not pretty if I don't get a little of both before the rest of the family wakes up. The whole day is thrown off if it's not started right.

Of course it's neither the coffee nor the quiet that gets me going in the morning. It's the time spent seeking the kingdom of God. Just by making an attempt to meet him in the pre-dawn stillness, he blesses me with "all these things."

Jesus never said, "find the kingdom of God." He simply said "seek it." There are many mornings when I haven't found anything at all. I can barely keep my eyes open and my thoughts focused on his word. But he blesses my intentions nonetheless and adds patience, love, joy, and countless other gifts to my day.

This holds true for my children as well. My oldest daughter dragged herself to her desk this morning, not exactly in the right frame of mind for lessons. (Murmurs of a sister wearing the shirt she wanted to wear were heard under her breath. Yes, even home-educated girls have occasional fashion "issues.") She opened her Bible to where we left off in 2 Timothy and rattled off the list of godless behaviors found in chapter 3. That was all she needed to bring her to a quick apology and a completely new attitude.

> For the word of God is living and active, sharper than any double-edged sword, it penetrates even to dividing soul and spirit, joints and marrow; it judges the thoughts and attitudes of the heart. (Hebrews 4:12)

The goal of Christian parenting is simple and comes straight from the word of God: "I have no greater joy than to hear that my children are walking in the truth" (3 John 4). I can't imagine any worldly prize greater than to know that my children love and serve the Lord. Everything else falls into place after that; there is no greater goal than to lead them right into the arms of the Savior. But how can they walk in the truth unless they know the truth? The world is not going to teach them. The world walks in darkness with willing abandon (Ephesians 4:17-32). It's been that way since the beginning of time, but before the age of reality television and in-your-face news coverage, it was easier to keep our eyes on the narrow path God has laid out for those who believe.

It's up to Christian parents to instill a love of God's word in the hearts of their children. Only the Spirit can make the seed grow and flourish in the life of your children, so a healthy dose of prayer should also go along with your family Bible reading. This reverence for the word begins, of course, with your own practice of "abiding" in him. If you've never had a discipline of daily quiet time, why not begin today? Starting your day with scripture will "guard your heart and mind in Christ Jesus" (Philippians 4:7) like nothing else. It's very difficult to feel overwhelmed, harried, and out-of-control after spending time with the one who calms the storms, carries our burdens, and who cares even about the hairs on our heads.

There is nothing quite so pleasing to the devil as Christians who think they don't need to stay rooted in God's word. If you need a refresher course on what happens to those who remain "planted by streams of water" versus those who go it alone, read Psalm 1. Jesus himself minces no words in his warning against this kind of "do it yourself" attitude:

> Remain in me, and I will remain in you. No branch can bear fruit by itself; it must remain in the vine. Neither can you bear fruit unless you remain in me... apart from me you can do nothing.
> (John 15:4-5)

Let me be clear: I've tried to go it alone. There have been seasons of discouragement or exhaustion — especially during pregnancy — when the last thing I wanted to do was pull myself out of bed early enough to have quiet time. My husband would dutifully throw off the covers and head straight to his Bible. Many days — many months — I have watched him go and simply rolled over, justifying my weakness in a million and one ways. While the time in bed may have been satisfying for a moment, my entire family would suffer as a result of my parched and drained spirit.

Thankfully, there have also been countless instances when Jesus has so extravagantly blessed my time with him in the early hours that I long to go back, morning by morning. Just yesterday, after journaling all he was teaching me from 1 Peter 2, I opened up Ann Voskamp's *One Thousand Gifts Devotional*. The day's reading was titled, "Hunting Grace." She tells of how a simple gift from her husband — a few pots from a thrift store — has turned the whole family into beauty hunters: "Have vessel. Now must find beauty."[1] Her children scramble to find flowers and other evidences of the Father's love to put in those empty vessels. My mind raced to farmers' markets, nature's bounty, and dinner menus and "Shouldn't I display flowers on our table more often?"

Not an hour later, my own children came rushing in with a package left at our doorstep. Flowers — at 8:30 a.m.! Were they from my husband? Not this time. They were from an anonymous sweet soul in our congregation who took the time to say, "All you do is appreciated. God bless you and your lovely family." Praise you, Jesus! Is it not enough that your word touches me, changes me, pursues me, and lavishes me with love? You add "grace upon grace" just to show me you're paying attention (John 1:16). Give me eyes to see, Lord. Keep me abiding in you so that I never fail to comprehend how you pursue me with your relentless love. How much have I missed on those days when I failed to meet you in your word.

As the years go by, I see the fruit of our efforts to instill his word in the hearts of our children come to blessed fruition. The children's "count it all joy" (James 1:2) begins to be muttered under my breath when the day is getting long, the fussiness is wearing on my soul, the dinner needs to be made, and another load of laundry must be put away. It's another coping mechanism — like the Kyrie — this knowledge that even the trials and tribulations are to be considered joy in the big picture. But my children know that one too many "count it all joys" means Mama isn't happy and things are going south very quickly.

On one such recent afternoon, after a particularly difficult morning at home, my daughter left me a reminder on the refrigerator door: "Children are a heritage from the Lord, the fruit of the womb, a reward" (Proverbs 127:3). She gets it. She knows. She's come to understand that sometimes her mom misses the big picture and needs to be reassured by his perfect, timely, and life-giving word. And for that I have no greater joy.

Spending Time in the Word Together

We have found different resources to be especially helpful through the seasons of our children's lives. Picture Bibles are perfect when children are little; not only do they teach the classic stories of God's people, they refresh your understanding of salvation history as a whole. By reading the Bible as an overarching narrative, you get the benefit of seeing the big picture. Our favorites are The Beginner's Bible and the NIRV Read With Me Bible (especially for young boys). Both have cartoonish illustrations that delight young minds. As your children get older, and their attention spans expand, Arthur Maxwell's *The Bible Story* takes them from Creation to Revelation with pictures (outdated but still nice for little eyes) in an easy, storytelling format. It's no small undertaking: ten volumes make up the set. However, it's an adequate bridge between the simple "hit the highlights" picture Bibles and the real deal. The Golden Children's Bible is also a treasure — beautiful language and equally impressive illustrations. In addition, we have found *Leading Little Ones to God* indispensable in terms of the basic theology necessary to answer the endless questions that spring forth "out of the mouths of babes" (Psalm 8:2). There is nothing quite like discussing the deep truths of God with the under six set over a bowl of ice cream right before bed.

The most important thing about having a family Bible time is having a family Bible time. We often feel discouraged after a particularly uproarious session, when one child is hanging upside down from the couch and another is drawing all over himself with Crayolas (or Sharpies® if it's been that kind of day). My pastor husband has been known to lament that "he can't even lead his own children in devotions." We trust that even on those less-than-perfect instances, God will bless our efforts. In the very least, our children will remember that ours is a family that reads the Bible together.

Again, the Lord promises no timetable for when your children will turn to his word on their own. The oft-quoted proverb promises, "train a child in the way he should go, and when he is old, he will not turn from it" (Proverbs 22:6). God is faithful. In his own time he will finish the good work you've begun. Recently, I asked my oldest daughter, now thirteen, what she does while she waits for her dad to finish up at church on those Sundays she stays late. Admittedly, I was fully expecting her to tell me about all the latest Instagram posts or something cute she found on Pinterest. I was delightfully mistaken: "I read my Bible and then pray in the Columbarium." Count it all joy!

---

1. Ann Voskamp, *One Thousand Gifts Devotional* (Grand Rapids: Zondervan, 2012), p. 81.

CHAPTER FOUR

Living the New Life: The Gift of Baptism

God has a thing for water. He covered the majority of his creation with oceans, lakes, and seas. He used water as the primary ingredient in the pinnacle of his creative endeavors: man. Water — the most abundant and necessary element on earth — was an integral part of God's salvation story from the very start: "In the beginning God created the heavens and the earth... and the Spirit of God was hovering over the waters" (Genesis 1:1-2). He chose water to cleanse the earth in the time of Noah. He used water to help the Israelites escape from the mighty Egyptians during the Exodus. Jesus turned water into wine in the very first miracle of his ministry at the wedding of Cana. Never mind that water has no nutritional value, no calories, no fat, no vitamins — without water we can't survive. There's something powerful, life-giving, and essential about water.

So when Jesus says he's the living water, he's saying our spirits can't thrive — they can't truly live — without him: "Whoever drinks the water I give him will never thirst. Indeed, the water I give him will become in him a spring welling up to eternal life" (John 4:14). Jesus spoke these words to a lost and lonely woman one day under the Mediterranean midday sun. She was tired. She was parched. No matter how many times she returned to this very same spot, no matter how many times she filled this very same bucket, the deep thirst within her was never satisfied.

Life had beaten her down by the time she met Jesus that day. Marriage hadn't worked out for her, at least not the way she had dreamed about as a little girl. It's not that she hadn't given it a chance. She'd had five husbands by this point and was quickly moving on to number six. It's that she was hoping some man had something — anything — that would take away the bitterness settling in her soul. She begged the one man who would talk to her at the well for a cure: "Sir, give me this water so that I won't get thirsty and have to keep coming here to draw water" (John 4:15).

Jesus, always one to do "more than we can ask or imagine" (Ephesians 3:20), gave her what she most desired: the truth. He called her out. He knew her, he knew all about her. His words — piercing as they were — washed over her like spring rain. For the first time, she understood that her shame wasn't enough to keep the living water from satisfying her weary and parched soul.

When the living water floods us with his grace, we are forever changed. Our shame and guilt and fear and loneliness are washed away because we've finally met our match. In Jesus, we finally find someone who knows us — everything about us — and still loves us. The woman at the well had lived with the shame of her past for so long that Jesus' words came not as rebuke but as pure relief. Seeing right into her soul was what convinced her that he alone could save her: "Come, see a man who told me everything I ever did. Could this be the Christ?" (John 4:29). That day, the Samaritan woman received grace upon grace from the living water himself: a clean heart, a new life, and a powerful testimony. Her story turned many hearts to Jesus, for "many of the Samaritans from that town believed in him because of the woman's testimony" (John 4:39).

A clean heart, a new life, and a powerful testimony — that's the business of baptism.

In the waters of baptism we die with Christ and rise to new life. We are given new birth, our sins are washed away, we are sealed by the Holy Spirit, and we are adopted into God's own family — we become his children. The words of a traditional baptismal liturgy beautifully remind us of all that happens when are baptized:

> In Holy Baptism our gracious heavenly Father liberates us from sin and death by joining us to the death and resurrection of our Lord Jesus Christ. We are born children of a fallen humanity; in the waters of baptism we are reborn children of God and inheritors of eternal life. By water and the Holy Spirit we are made members of the church which is the Body of Christ. As we live with him and with his people, we grow in faith, love, and obedience to the will of God.
> (*Lutheran Book of Worship*, p. 121)

We baptize not only because of all the great blessings baptism bestows on us, but first and foremost because Jesus commands us to: "Go therefore, and make disciples of all nations, baptizing them in the name of the Father, and of the Son, and of the Holy Spirit" (Matthew 28:19). Baptism is a sacrament: a special means of grace where God promises to be with us in a different and tangible way. In light of all this, then, when people ask, "Do I have to be baptized?" the church replies, "Why wouldn't you want to be?"

To be sure, baptism is not an insurance policy into heaven or a get-out-of-jail-free card. It's the beginning of a relationship. Our sinful nature wants to boil down our salvation to the lowest common denominator: as Lutherans, we emphasize being saved by faith; Catholics by works; and Evangelicals by belief. The Bible teaches us they all go together. Salvation is a multivariable equation: it's not just baptism, just faith, or just works. God's word says we are "saved by" a long list of things including: believing, repentance, baptism, the work of the Spirit, declaring with our mouths, works, grace, his blood, his righteousness, and his cross.

God can and does change us in a variety of ways through a variety of means. But it's in baptism that he promises to change us. Not many of us would refuse such a fresh start. God graciously lets us begin again at the baptismal font: "We are born children of a fallen humanity, in the waters of baptism we are reborn children of God and inheritors of eternal life." Through water and the Spirit, God wipes the slate clean. We don't have to stay the same. We are born again.

Such a Refuge Ne'er Was Given

At the church I grew up in, we sang "Children Of The Heavenly Father" at every baptism. I still know all the words by heart; each of the four verses is my favorite. The simple truth that God takes care of his own was deeply ingrained on my heart as a child: "God his own doth tend and nourish, in his holy courts they flourish. From all evil things he spares them, in this mighty arms he bears them." There was something very beautiful and special about baptism Sundays: the baby all in white, the adoring parents, the extended family looking a little uncomfortable sitting in the first pew for all to see.

Such occasions in your own church provide great opportunities to remind your children what God does for each of us in baptism. If you belong to a church that baptizes infants, your children will be awed by the fact that one day not so long ago it was them up there in the pastor's arms. Many families celebrate their child's baptismal day each year by lighting a candle, having a special meal, or taking time to thank God for welcoming each of us into his family through baptism. My parents dutifully send my children cards on their baptismal birthdays, another simple way of reminding them that something special happened when God's grace was literally poured out for them.

I want my children to have a deep sense of belonging to Christ and to his bride, the church. I want them to never know life without the love, support, and accountability that a church family provides. Baptism is initiation into "so great a cloud of witnesses" (Hebrews 12:1). It's the beginning of a beautiful relationship: clean heart, new life, powerful testimony.

CHAPTER FIVE

Living in Communion: The Gift of Forgiveness

It had been a long day already and we hadn't even had lunch yet. My unsuspecting four-year-old was playing with Monopoly® pieces in a ceramic pitcher in the kitchen as I prepared lunch. Sure enough, the pitcher fell off the shelf and crashed into hundreds of shards all over the floor.

I wish this had been one of those "let's don't cry over spilled milk" situations that occur constantly in a busy household. I wish I had handled it with grace and patience.

I didn't.

I lost it. Right there in the middle of the kitchen in the middle of the day. I yelled, I screamed, and I used "bad language." My son slumped into the living room, hid on the couch, and began licking his wounds. And I don't mean only the proverbial ones I'd just inflicted in my complete overreaction. I mean the real ones that occurred because the pitcher landed on his foot. I was so busy being upset over yet another disaster on an already miserable day that I didn't even notice my boy was bleeding.

It pains me to write about such an embarrassing loss of self-control; not because I worry what someone may think of me, but because I know that these lapses are also part of our family story. We fail one another each and every day. There are hurt feelings, injustices, and cruel words suffered by all of us at one another's expense. Sin — it certainly exists within the walls of this particular home.

"If we truly want peace in the world, let us begin by loving one another in our own families," said Mother Teresa.[1]

The reality is that the home is experienced by many as a battleground, a lost cause, a place to let our worst selves reign unfettered. A horrifying article about domestic violence in my local paper read, "These cases are a reminder that the home is not a safe place for all Americans and that people do the unthinkable each day against people they say they love."[2] It can't be so for those who choose to follow Jesus: "As God's chosen people, holy and dearly loved, clothe yourselves with compassion, kindness, humility, gentleness, and patience. Bear with each other and forgive whatever grievances you may have against one another. Forgive as the Lord forgave you. And over all these virtues put on love, which binds them all together in perfect unity" (Colossians 3:12-14). My husband and I chose those very words to be read at our wedding; they describe the love and forgiveness we strive to characterize in our home.

Forgiveness doesn't come naturally to me. I don't often want to ask for it and I'm equally reluctant to give it. I can hold a grudge with the best of them. It's a bad place to be because Jesus tells me that I will be forgiven to the same extent I forgive. "... If you do not forgive men their sins, your Father will not forgive your sins" (Matthew 6:15). And if there's one thing that does come naturally to me it is sin. I have to choose forgiveness — every — single — day.

After I had my little temper tantrum that fateful day in the kitchen, I walked over to where my son lay holding his foot. "Did the pitcher cut you?" I asked meekly. He nodded. "Can I have a look?" Another nod. I wrapped my arms around him and told him how wrong I was to lose my temper over such a little thing. I looked into his big brown eyes, said that I was sorry, and that I hoped he could forgive me. Another nod and a little head buried in my shoulder. We tended his wounds — both inside and out. A relationship was restored.

"The home is the first school of the Christian life where

all learn love, repeated forgiveness, and prayerful worship," according to the catechism of the Catholic church. Love, forgiveness, and prayer: they all go together. Love requires forgiveness and forgiveness often comes only through prayer. The family should be a safe place to work through these things and grow in the gifts that come only by the power of God's Spirit: "love, joy, peace, patience, kindness, goodness, faithfulness, gentleness, and self-control" (Galatians 5:22). Modeling forgiveness to our children — when we need it and when we need to give it — is the only way to ensure they will learn to "forgive, as they have been forgiven" (Ephesians 4:32).

How Beautiful Is the Body of Christ

Joseph and his brothers — all twelve of them — suffered more than your average amount of sibling rivalry. The older boys, jealous about a jacket their father had given Joseph and tired of hearing him drone on about his crazy dreams, decided the only way to deal with their little brother was to kill him: "Come now, let's kill him and throw him into one of these cisterns and say that a ferocious animal devoured him" (Genesis 37:20). After throwing him into the pit, they promptly sat down to a nice picnic on the side of the road and forgot about their own flesh and blood. Judah, beginning to feel a little bit guilty, decided instead to sell Joseph off to the first traveling caravan to pass by, which happened to be the Ishmaelites. He ended up pocketing twenty shekels on the deal. So much for brotherly love.

As the years passed things went very well for Joseph. He rose to a high position in Egypt, becoming second in command to Pharaoh and enjoying all the riches of the kingdom. His brothers, on the other hand, were barely scraping by in Shechem because of a wide-reaching famine. Long story short, Joseph's brothers traveled to Egypt to beg for grain. They did not recognize their little brother Joseph, who was in charge. He most certainly recognized them. After all they had done to him, he rolled out the royal carpet, set a table before them — a feast in a time of famine — and forgave them: "You intended to harm me, but God intended it for good" (Genesis 50:19).

Joseph not only set the table for his brothers, he set the stage for Jesus. Despite being despised and rejected, despite having one of his own betray him, Jesus set a feast before his friends at the Last Supper. He took the bread, broke it, and told them it was his body, given for them. He took the cup, poured the wine, and said it was his blood poured out for the forgiveness of sins: "This is my body, given for you. This is my blood, shed for you. Do this, for the remembrance of me" (Luke 22:19).

When we come to the Lord's Table we do so knowing that we don't deserve the gift he's giving us. We've taken so many wrong turns, we've turned our backs on him so many times. We prefer to be left in the pit of our sin and apathy, rather then let our brother, Jesus Christ, restore us to right relationship with our holy and heavenly Father. Yet his words draw us back, time and time again: "Take and eat, this is my body. Take and drink, this is my blood. Do this, for the forgiveness of sins." As we kneel at the altar, the depth of his love for us overshadows our own little problems and preoccupations. Being back in the light of God's love lifts up our hearts and moves us beyond ourselves. It reminds us to forgive as we have been forgiven.

Communion with Children

Many churches encourage formal instruction before allowing children to take communion. In the Catholic church, this happens around second grade. In my Lutheran tradition, we wait until fifth grade to instruct young people about the Sacrament of the Altar. Regardless of your church's age recommendations, the scriptures are clear that taking the Lord's Supper without an understanding of what it means is irresponsible, even detrimental: "For anyone who eats and drinks without recognizing the body of the Lord eats and drinks judgment on himself" (1 Corinthians 11:29). This is why some denominations exclude people from partaking in the Lord's Supper if they aren't members of the church. On the surface this practice rubs people the wrong way, "Why exclude anyone from the gift of forgiveness found in the Eucharist?" The principle behind it is more protective than prohibitive, however; these churches want to make sure no one "eats and drinks judgment on himself" (1 Corinthians 11:29).

Generally speaking, children readily accept the mystery of the bread and wine becoming Jesus' body and blood. I've heard it explained to young people in satisfyingly simple terms. We don't see the Vitamin C in an orange. We don't even taste it. But we know it's there not only because someone told us so, but because we experience its nourishment and healthy benefits. The same can be said of the elements of communion. We don't see his body and blood — or how they're in there — but we experience them powerfully as we take the bread and the wine. "How many of you say: I should like to see his face, his garments, his shoes. You do see him, you touch him, you eat him. He gives himself to you, not only that you may see him, but also to be your food and nourishment."[3] *Eucharisteo!* Thank you, Jesus.

A Clean Heart

David knew what forgiveness felt like. He hadn't lived

a perfect life, not by a long shot. After an adulterous affair, he sent his mistress' husband to the front lines of battle to be killed. A great deal of family drama and pain resulted from David's transgressions. Rather than running away from his past, David knew he needed God. He never gave up his relentless pursuit of the only one who could forgive his sins. He chased after God like a thirsty animal, "as a deer pants for streams of water, so my soul pants for you, O God" (Psalm 42:1).

After finding peace through a completely restored relationship with God, David was free to forgive others. His beautiful song of confession and forgiveness is used in liturgies throughout the world as an everlasting testimony to God's goodness and mercy: "Create in me a pure heart, O God, and renew a steadfast spirit within me. Do not cast me from your presence or take your Holy Spirit from me. Restore to me the joy of your salvation" (Psalm 51:10-11). When God does indeed restore him, then, and only then, can David turn God's love outward, to a world in desperate need of forgiveness: "Then I will teach transgressors your ways, and sinners will turn back to you" (Psalm 51:13). Jesus calls us to do the same: "freely you have received, freely give" (Matthew 10:8).

---

1. As quoted in "Mother Teresa Reflects on Working Toward Peace," The Jesuit University in Silicon Valley, http://www.scu.edu/ethics/architects-of-peace/Teresa/essay.html.

2. Jesse Washington, "Surge of Grisly Killings Has People Asking Why," *Columbus Dispatch*, November 2, 2013.

3. St. John Chrysostom as quoted in Andrew Purves, *Pastoral Theology in the Classical Tradition* (Westminster: John Knox Press, 2001), p. 42.

CHAPTER SIX

Living with Purpose: The Gift of God's Best

God doesn't want what's good for your family. He wants what's best. There's a big difference. So much of what's out there is good: sports, clubs, academic enrichment — you can have your children scheduled from sun up to sun down with good things. But would that be the best for them? More importantly, would it be best for your family? Into the chaos and confusion of all that clamors for our attention, God calmly offers something better: "I will show you a still more excellent way" (1 Corinthians 12:31).

There are defining moments in most of our lives that make us stop, take stock of where we are and where we want to be, and we make the necessary changes. Sometimes those are major life events, like the death of a parent or the loss of a job. Sometimes those are seemingly small circumstances that gently turn us in another direction.

When it came time for my oldest daughter to attend preschool, we signed her up excitedly — just like everyone else did. She picked out a backpack, found her cubby, and happily joined her new friends a few mornings a week at a local church. Preschools — in all of their pint-sized precociousness — make a parent's heart swell. Everything is just so bright and cheerful — what's not to love?

At the time, we lived in Fargo, North Dakota. Below freezing temperatures were not altogether unusual in the early weeks of the school year. When the wind chill was just beginning to bite, I had baby number three to consider as I chauffeured my little scholar to and from her newly-budding academic career. Not only did this require bundling up a tiny boy and his not-much-older sisters — a monumental task in and of itself — it also demanded breaking parenting commandment #1: never wake a sleeping baby. Instead of snuggling in for stories while the baby napped, we donned our Arctic gear and headed out to face the frost.

Of course that wasn't our main problem. My daughters, who have always been best friends, were having "issues" at the onset of preschool. The one left at home was jealous that her sister was having fabulous adventures without her. The one at preschool was feeling left out of the fun we had at home in her absence. It always took a considerable amount of time for them to re-acclimate to life "as it used to be." We'd stagger in from preschool pick-up, shed our layers of winter necessities and backpacks and papers (all over the house). I would then attempt to get my baby down for a nap while making lunch and dealing with squabbling sisters. This was not the bright and cheerful routine I'd signed up for. I was beginning to have serious misgivings: my four-year-old's academic adventures were quickly holding our previously-happy-little-life hostage.

Not wanting to give up too easily, though, we signed on for another year. Honestly, I was a little ashamed that no one else complained about the "preschool grind." How bad could it be? Everyone else did it. But by the second year, adding to my misgivings was the fact that my daughter was coming home with some not-so-bright-and-cheerful habits. When I'd ask her to put her things away, she'd purposefully ignore me; later claiming that if you don't do what you're supposed to do when you're asked, you'll get a sticker for doing it later. Whoa, Nelly! "The kids who don't listen get stickers when they do listen?" Let's just say that when the kindergarten bus rolled around the following September, our daughter wasn't on it.

That's the very short version of how God led us into home education (we also spent a considerable amount of time in prayer regarding how best to educate our children). This isn't a chapter on school choice, it's about seeking out and responding to God's best for your family. It's about not settling for "good" when he's calling you to something better — whatever that means for your particular family. God called our family to a non-traditional path of education. While it's hasn't always been easy, he has guided us every step of the way and we see his fingerprints all over this often-overwhelming endeavor. For other families, it's something completely different. The point is that God will nudge you in the direction he wants you to go. When you have the courage to follow, he'll be there blessing you every step of the way: "Trust in the Lord with all your heart and lean not on your own understanding; in all your ways acknowledge him, and he will make your paths straight" (Proverbs 3:5-6).

Cameron Townsend, the founder of Wycliffe Bible Translators, spent ten years of his life writing an alphabet for the Cakchiquel Indians in Mexico and then translating the New Testament into their own language. Many people became followers of Jesus Christ because of his amazingly powerful ministry. Townsend was doing a whole lot of good for the Lord. It wasn't enough. He desired to live God's best. He wanted other people — hundreds of them — to have access to the word of God too. Many of his colleagues discouraged him, saying he needed to stay with the Cakchiquel and continue to shepherd them himself. After much prayer, Townsend felt God calling him through the words of Jesus, "Suppose one of you has a hundred sheep and loses one of them. Does he not leave the ninety-nine in the open country and go after the lost sheep until he finds it?" (Luke 15:4). Townsend believed God's best for his life was to go after the one, rather than staying with the 99. He listened to the Lord.

Because of his faithfulness, Wycliffe has translated the Bible into hundreds of languages all over the world. Because of Townsend's obedience, thousands of previously unreached people have come to know the Lord Jesus.

Many of the choices God calls us to make on behalf of our families are countercultural and they aren't always well received. Some of them will be met with disapproval from well-meaning friends and family members. Following Jesus means carrying our crosses, even when they're awkward and difficult to handle. Something as simple as ensuring that your family has a few evenings each week with nothing on the schedule is an act of serious restraint in this frenetic culture. Just yesterday, as I waited to pick up my daughter from gymnastics, I heard some of the parents complaining about how they have no free evenings this fall. This fall? As in, the entire season?

As I thought about their conversation on our drive home, I realized they weren't actually complaining. They were one-upping each other with their busy schedules. I have six active children and a husband in ministry. I can manage a harried, frantic pace like the best of them for a week or two — but a season? Count me out! I don't have it in me to sustain that kind of pace for any length of time. I'm pretty sure it's not in the best interest of those around me either.

God is serious when he says, "Come to me all you who are weary and burdened, and I will give you rest" (Matthew 11:28). I don't know too many parents who aren't both weary and burdened. It comes with the territory, but certainly not to the extent our culture encourages. The latest energy drinks are marketed not to athletes and students but to busy moms on the go. As if the pretty pink packaging of Flirt™ and Bloom Energy™ would transform the harried housewife into a She-Ra of domestic dominance. As if that's what the world-weary mom needs. I'm all for a nice jolt of caffeine once in a while, but when it comes to a source of strength for the journey, I'll take the Lord's living water over Bloom Energy™ any day of the week.

In the best scenarios, the home provides a peaceful place to refresh, regroup, and re-enter the world God calls us to love and to serve. Our homes are our arks in a world flooded with noise and negativity. They provide a place to experience one of God's greatest gifts: restoration. He alone "restores our souls" (Psalm 23:3). Managing eternal souls — the job description of Christian parenting — strikes me as fairly serious business. It requires more than we've got. It requires God. Unfortunately, many of us are so busy keeping busy, we fail to hear God calling us to something different. Choosing God's best instead of the world's good requires intentionality. It demands following the path that God is laying out for your family, not the one everyone else is traveling. It requires living with purpose: "And we know that in all things God works for the good of those who love him, who have been called according to his purpose" (Romans 8:28).

CHAPTER SEVEN

Living a Family Culture: The Gift of Doing Things Differently

When God formed the nation of Israel, he did so through one man: Abraham. Abraham and his wife Sarah had no children when God promised to make Abraham "a great nation" (Genesis 12:2). God took Abraham outside one night and said, "Look up at the heavens and count the stars — if indeed you can count them... so shall your offspring be" (Genesis 15:5). God super-sized Abraham's family thousands of years ago so that they could make a super-sized difference in the world. This was the original "pay it forward" plan. God blessed this one family so that they could go on to bless others: "all the peoples on the earth will be blessed through you" (Genesis 12:3).

God gave the Israelites — Abraham's family — an incredibly long list of dos and don'ts to ensure that they would be very different from all the other nations around them. The over-six-hundred commandments in the Old Testament set the Israelites apart from all their neighbors. They had their own way of talking, dressing, eating, worshiping, farming, and even resting. You knew an Israelite when you saw one because Abraham's family had its own culture.

Every family — whether big or small — has a culture. It's the DNA of how the family operates. A family culture may be positive or negative. It may be clearly defined or established only by default. Regardless, experts agree that "family culture plays a more important role in shaping a child than parenting styles."[1] As Christians, we strive to create a family culture that is recognizably different than our non-believing counterparts.

All Christians have come into God's family the same way: through adoption. When we accept Jesus as our Lord and Savior, God welcomes us into his very own family. He calls us his children; he becomes our Father. "I will be a Father to you, and you will be my sons and daughters, says the Lord almighty" (2 Corinthians 6:18). We should, then, bear a family resemblance to his only "true" Son, Jesus. It is through this family relationship that we become more like him and less like us. We grow. We change. We begin to radiate his love: "the light of the righteous shines brightly" (Proverbs 13:9). Our lives often take radically different paths than those prescribed by our upbringing or education. Those who "knew us when" wonder what in the world happened.

Plenty of people wonder that about me.

I gave my life to the Lord as a preteen at a Young Life Camp in Minnesota. It took me many more years, though, to begin walking in his ways. When I got to Dartmouth College, God turned my world upside down through a campus ministry called The Navigators. As a college athlete, my afternoons and weekends were spent at the rink training with the women's hockey team. Sunday morning church wasn't an option. I started attending Tuesday Night Fellowship, a ministry sponsored by both The Navigators and Campus Crusade for Christ (now Cru). These young men and women were serious about the scriptures: they read them daily, memorized them proficiently, and applied them beautifully to their lives. Their peace and joy was palpable. I wanted what they had. Slowly but surely, my heart was finding its new home.

But I was still struggling in my walk with the Lord. I preferred my own way of doing things, thank you very much. I fell in love with a cute brown-eyed singer. Like most of my college friends and acquaintances, he didn't know the Lord.

We parted ways when he graduated: he, happy to be off on post-college adventures; me, heartbroken that God wouldn't allow me to "be yoked together with an unbeliever" (2 Corinthians 6:14). The fact that God brought this scripture to my attention and led me to obey was progress. It was also painful. Little did I know that God had big plans for both of us.

No one who knew us then would have predicted the life we live now: a home-educating pastor's family with six children and a twelve-passenger van. Who knew I'd be happily at home changing diapers for the thirteenth year in a row? Who could have dreamed we'd have an oversized family when many of our Ivy League friends — and a large percentage of Gen Xers — decided to forego marriage and family life entirely? We live on one income and we don't have cable TV. Yes, we're that family.

Christian families, like their Israelite counterparts, are called to be set apart: "You are a chosen people, a royal priesthood, a holy nation, a people belonging to God..." (1 Peter 2:9). Jesus may have freed us from the ritual laws regarding diet and daily life, but we remain bound by the Ten Commandments and the Golden Rule. Those alone, if truly practiced, go a long way in making your family a breath of fresh air in an increasingly stale and self-serving society. Christian families are to be recognized by what they do, "by their fruit you will recognize them" (Matthew 7:20); and by how they love, "by this all men will know that you are my disciple, if you love one another" (John 13:35).

Creating an atmosphere of "good fruit" and sacrificial love inside the home is the first step toward reaching out to the world with God's gift of grace and salvation. Our homes need to be built upon the solid rock of God's word instead of the sinking sand of the world's ways, "unless the Lord builds the house, its builders labor in vain" (Psalm 127:1). Laboring to create a home filled with all the fruits of God's Spirit

— love, joy, peace, patience, kindness, goodness, faithfulness, gentleness, and self-control — takes everything we've got. It requires making family and home life our number one priority. It demands denying our culture's "me first" mentality and putting our spouses and children before ourselves. Quite often it means deferring dreams in favor of discipling the next generation of world-changers.

Like Abraham, Christian families are blessed to be a blessing. We are saved to serve. We are called to live beyond ourselves, to let God use us in a suffering world. The reality in modern America is that we don't have to go further than our own neighborhoods to make a great difference for his kingdom. Wherever you live, many of your neighbors don't yet know the Lord. You're strategically positioned to make your home an embassy for Jesus in a "foreign land."

You don't have to go knocking on doors to share the gospel with your neighbors. You can bring their children to Vacation Bible School, or AWANA (Approved Workmen Are Not Ashamed), or to worship on Sunday. When neighbor children are at your home, you can include them in your family's Bible time. When yours is the only car leaving the street on Sunday mornings, your actions the rest of the week will speak volumes to a spiritually curious neighbor. Bringing baked goods to a widow near you or having your children secretly rake an elderly neighbor's lawn is a simple way to spread God's love beyond the walls of your "embassy." Practicing hospitality — even just having another family over for dinner — teaches your children about serving and putting other's needs before your own. There is nothing radical or difficult in any of these measures, but they are quickly becoming a lost art. In our 24/7 world, it's easy to the let busyness crowd out being a good neighbor. The hardest part is making the time to do such simple acts of service. Jesus said even "a cup of cold water" (Matthew 10:42) goes a long way to satisfy a parched and weary soul.

Shining Like Stars

One aspect of creating a distinctly Christian family culture is guarding our children's hearts. We're never going to be able to completely shelter our children from the crass and obnoxious culture that surrounds them at every turn. A simple internet search can go very wrong, very fast. The magazine rack at the grocery store checkout should assault everyone's sense of modesty, but we've become too desensitized to care. All of these everyday encounters illuminate how hard it is to shield our children from indecency. The first two groups of Halloween trick-or-treaters at my door — both sets strangers — assumed I'd have no problem with their less than appropriate initial impression. First, a group of prepubescent boys rang the doorbell and yelled (repeatedly), "twerk or treat!" As if the gyrating antics of a pop star are suitable conversation for anyone who crosses their path. The second set was a young couple with little children. The mother was introducing herself when the father piped in, "I'm just her concubine." I was already anticipating the inevitable, "What's a concubine, Mommy?" before I even closed the door. Now what? You can't easily keep the world out when it shows up at your doorstep.

Why should Christians even bother attempting to protect our children's innocence in a culture like ours? What's the use? The point is that our children's hearts — and our own — are God's property and his prized possession. We must shepherd them well. God admonishes us to keep his children "blameless and pure, children of God without fault in a crooked and depraved generation, in which you shine like stars in the universe as you hold out the word of life" (Philippians 2:15-16). He commands us to be set apart so that we have something to offer a broken world. God's love radiates from those who love him. It shines brightly on their faces because it spills out of their hearts. If people can't tell us apart from everyone else around us, we may need to re-evaluate how closely we're following our king. If we fail to distinguish ourselves from the surrounding culture, we don't have anything to offer. If we don't share the "word of life," we only add to the din of death all around us. And if we "hide our light under a bushel" (Matthew 5:15), we have no way of "shining like stars" (Philippians 2:15).

The world desperately needs what God alone offers: unconditional love, forgiveness of sins, and life everlasting. He calls us out of the darkness and into his glorious light — not just for our benefit, but so others can come out from the shadows as well. He wants our lives to reflect his light in a way that draws others to himself: "Let your light so shine before men, that they may see your good works and glorify your heavenly Father" (Matthew 5:16).

God desires that no one — not one person — be lost. He graciously invites our families to be a part of his great search and rescue mission in the world.

---

1. H. Brevy Cannon, *UVA Today*, "University of Virginia Study Identifies Four Family Cultures in America," November 15, 2012.

CHAPTER EIGHT

Living for the Lord: The Gift of Legacy

We want to do big things for the Lord. We want our lives to count for Christ. We want to make a difference in the world. We want to leave a legacy. We mistakenly define greatness the way the world does: by power, name recognition, or international influence. God has never seen it in those terms. In fact, he views success in a completely different way: "Whoever exalts himself will be humbled, and whoever humbles himself will be exalted" (Matthew 23:12). When we choose to humbly serve him in the areas he's already given us, then, and only then, does he trust us with greater spheres of influence: "You have been faithful with a few things; I will put you in charge of many things. Come and share your master's happiness!" (Matthew 25:23). Making the master happy with our stewardship of the "small things" — like the souls of our children — is the most meaningful influence anyone can have. If you are a parent, then God has already given you a magnificent calling. First and foremost, he's asking you to lead your children to him.

The first commandment God gave to Adam and Eve was "to be fruitful and multiply" (Genesis 1:28). He also told them to "fill the earth and subdue it" (Genesis 1:28). He wanted Adam and Eve to spread his influence throughout the world by raising their children to love and serve him. When the Israelites prepared to enter a new territory, God gave them the same message over and over again: "be fruitful and multiply." They obeyed God to such an extent that they became "exceedingly numerous" (Exodus 1:7). Nations began to "dread the Israelites" because of their sheer numbers (Exodus 1:12) and their resulting influence on a foreign culture.

God commands each and every generation to be faithful with the next, so that his kingdom will spread to the ends of the earth. God started with the family of Abraham. They multiplied and became the nation of Israel, which gave birth to the one who came for all: "every nation, tribe, people, and language" (Revelation 7:9). God works from the inside out. When Jesus told his disciples to go spread the word, he told them to start at home: first to Jerusalem, then out to Judea, and finally "to the ends of the earth" (Acts 1:8). You can't win the world without first winning the hearts at home.

Many of us get so caught up leading others to Christ that we lose sight of our own. We strive for "greatness" in the kingdom of God when he's primarily calling us to the little people living right under our feet. Jesus warns us about this faulty focus: "What good is it for a man to gain the whole world, yet forfeit his soul?" (Mark 8:36). I don't want to gain anything if it means losing one of my little ones' souls.

Make no mistake, your children will either be for Jesus or against him. There is no middle ground: "He who is not with me is against me" (Matthew 12:30). If there's anything to be aggressive about in this lifetime, it's how intentionally we shape our children. God is calling us to win the next generation for him. The family has always been the place to do that.

From the beginning, God instructed his people to diligently teach their children the ways of the Lord:

> Fix these words of mine in your hearts and minds; tie them as symbols on your hands and bind them on your foreheads. Teach them to your children, talking about them when you sit at home and when

you walk along the road, when you lie down and when you get up. Write them on the doorframes of your houses and on your gates, so that your days and the days of your children may be many in the land that the Lord swore to give your ancestors, as many as the days that the heavens are above the earth.
(Deuteronomy 11:18-21)

God knew his children would encounter a wide variety of worldviews and a plethora of unfamiliar practices in their wanderings throughout the world. We think our culture has "gone to hell in a hand basket," but they were dealing with child sacrifice and temple prostitution! God knew it would take more than a Bible study here or a worship service there to counter the constant attacks to their way of life. As a result, he commanded them to do more. He commanded them to live their faith.

God commands the same of us today, "And whatever you do, whether in word or in deed, do it all in the name of the Lord Jesus, giving thanks to God the Father through him" (Colossians 3:17). Whatever you do — whether it's cleaning floors or helping with homework or pushing a little one in the swing — do it in the name of Jesus. That's the kind of faith that's contagious. It's authentic, it flows from the heart, it calls others to come along.

People say that real faith is "more caught than taught." That may be true to some extent: When our children see us pray in a time of stress, or serve in a time of need, they learn to do the same. I'm constantly amazed at how quickly even my littlest ones learn to fold their tiny hands and bow their tiny heads at mealtime. Or how my four year old will remind me to pray when I'm obviously concerned about something. They do "catch" on. But if we want our children to move beyond "milk" and onto the "solid food" of God's word, we need to diligently and intentionally teach them (1 Corinthians 3:2).

God alone can call our children to himself. It's only through his Spirit that they will come to believe and put their trust in him. But we have the great privilege and responsibility of tending the soil of their souls, ensuring that when the seed of God's word falls on them, it will grow and flourish and produce a good crop, "a hundred, sixty, or thirty times what was sown" (Matthew 13:8).

A Lasting Legacy

When embarking on a mission of importance, experts will tell you to "begin with the end in mind." As Christian parents, what is "the end"? Children who love and serve the Lord. Yes, and then some. We pray that our children's children will also walk in his ways. We pray that God's blessing will extend "to a thousand generations" (Exodus 20:6). We pray for a lasting legacy.

My husband recently attended the funeral service for the father of one of our friends. This man had six children, just as we do. As the family processed down the aisle, my husband was immediately struck by the visual of this man's legacy: his children, their spouses, and the numerous grandchildren were a beautiful testament to God's faithfulness. They took up many rows in the sanctuary; they had obviously "increased in number" (Genesis 1:28). Their influence was great. We often forget, in the many details and distractions of daily life with children, just how much God can do with small acts of obedience on our part.

Naaman was a man of great influence in the ancient kingdom of Aram: "He was a great man in the sight of his master and highly regarded" (2 Kings 5:1). He was a valiant soldier and the Lord had given victory to Aram because of him. But he had one fairly large problem. He had leprosy.

He also had a young girl in his household who knew the Lord. Naaman's wife's servant happened to be an Israelite. She told Naaman to go "see the prophet in Samaria" (2 Kings 5:3) because he could cure him. When Naaman met the prophet Elisha, he didn't like the terms of the healing. Elisha asked him to wash in the Jordan River seven times. Naaman thought that was far too simple. He wanted something big, something flashy, something that would dazzle the crowd: "I thought he would surely come out to me and stand and call on the name of their Lord his God, wave his hand over the spot and cure me of my leprosy" (2 Kings 5:11).

Luckily for Naaman, he had some very wise servants advising him, "If the prophet had told you to do some great thing, would you not have done it? How much more should you do, then, when he tells you, 'wash and be cleansed!' " (2 Kings 5:13). Naaman was willing to do something difficult as long as it looked good. But to do something simple — something right before him — where's the glory in that?

Sometimes it's easier to trust in the "great things" claiming our time and energy than the simple ones staring us right in the face every day. Sometimes it's easier to spend ourselves in the service of the world — our jobs, our commitments, our communities — than in sacrifice for those most dear to us. As Christian parents, we often lose sight of the magnificent claim upon our lives, forgetting that "there is no higher height to which humanity can attain than that occupied by a converted, heaven-inspired, praying [parent]."[1] It's often the littlest acts of obedience — the ones that occur right in our own homes — that go the farthest in serving our Lord.

May God bless you and yours, generation after generation.

1. Elizabeth Eliot, *The Shaping of a Christian Family* (Ada, Michigan: Revell, 2005).

www.ingramcontent.com/pod-product-compliance
Lightning Source LLC
Chambersburg PA
CBHW071757040426
42446CB00012B/2594